# THE LITTLE BOOK OF
# LIVERPOOL

Independent and Unofficial

FIFTH EDITION

**EDITED BY**
**GEOFF TIBBALS**

**CARLTON**
**BOOKS**

First published by Carlton Books in 2002
Reprinted with updates in 2003, 2004, 2005, 2007, 2008, 2009,
Second edition 2010, 2011, 2012
Third edition 2013
Fourth edition 2014, 2015, 2016
Fifth edition 2017
Reprinted in 2018

Carlton Books Limited
20 Mortimer Street
London W1T 3JW

A CIP catalogue record of this book is available from the British Library.

ISBN  978 1 78097 966 3

Printed in Dubai

# CONTENTS

# INTRODUCTION

Bill Shankly, Tommy Smith, the Kop – the history of Liverpool Football Club is rich in colourful characters who have never been short of a sharp one-liner. You only have to look at the number of ex-Liverpool players who have become TV pundits. To think, Alan Hansen was criticised by his former manager for not having enough to say for himself!

Alongside the shafts of Scouse and Scottish wit, this book contains more serious quotes offering rare insights into the private lives and careers of the players and management staff who have graced Anfield. So if you want to know what it means to join Liverpool, play at Anfield or what Paul Ince rates as better than sex, read on.

# CHAPTER 1

# THE LIVERPOOL WAY

**"**When you have a Liverpool shirt on your back as part of the squad, you will do anything to make sure you preserve what it stands for.**"**

**GERARD HOULLIER**

**❝**From my first day at Melwood,
I appreciated Liverpool's
special DNA. **❞**

**JOHN BARNES**

**"**This record sums up our spirit on the field. No player in my team struggles or battles alone. There's always someone there to help him.**"**

**BILL SHANKLY**

*discussing 'You'll Never Walk Alone'*

**"**Mind, I've been here during the bad times too. One year we came second. **"**

**BOB PAISLEY**

**❝**Liverpool Football Club is all about winning things and being a source of pride to our fans. It has no other purpose.**❞**

**DAVID MOORES**

*Honorary Life President of Liverpool Football Club*

**"**The only way to beat Liverpool is to let the ball down. **"**

*Portsmouth manager* **ALAN BALL**

**❝** The people who come to watch
us play, who love the team and regard it as
part of their lives, would never appreciate
Liverpool having a huge balance in the bank.
They want every asset we possess to be
wearing a red shirt. **❞**

**KENNY DALGLISH**

**"**It's there to remind our lads who they're playing for, and to remind the opposition who they're playing against.**"**

**BILL SHANKLY**

*explaining the significance of the 'This Is Anfield' plaque*

**"** Liverpool had dug its claws ever deeper into our psyche until, at all times, the craving to be simply the best lay just below the surface. **"**

**ALAN EDGE**

*Faith of our Fathers*

**❝**You get to wish that they would just occasionally pass the ball to the other team, like the rest of us do. **❞**

*Watford boss* **GRAHAM TAYLOR**

*despairing of playing Liverpool*

**❝** The Liverpool philosophy is simple, and is based on total belief. Maybe that has been the key to Liverpool's consistency. We were taught to go out there, play our own game and fear no one. **❞**

**PHIL NEAL**

**"**It's always a great honour for me to captain this football club.**"**

**JAMES MILNER**

**"** Anfield without European football
is like a banquet without wine. **"**

**ROY EVANS**

**❝**Liverpool has always been about winning, but it's also about the style. Over time we'll look to put that in place at all levels.**❞**

**BRENDAN RODGERS**

**❝**It's a magical, magical feeling to walk on to this pitch and think that we are the new owners.**❞**

**JOHN W. HENRY**

*stepping out at Anfield*

❝What attracts you to this club is its history. If you are clever and bright enough, you will look into the history.❞

**BRENDAN RODGERS**

# CHAPTER 2

# SHANKLY'S SAYINGS

**❝**There are two great teams
in Liverpool: Liverpool and
Liverpool Reserves. **❞**

**BILL SHANKLY**

**If** Everton were playing at the bottom of my garden, I'd draw the curtains. **"**

**BILL SHANKLY**

**❝**Don't worry, Alan. You'll be playing near a great side.**❞**

**BILL SHANKLY**

*to Alan Ball after he joined Everton*

**66** I know this is a sad occasion but I think that Dixie would be amazed to know that even in death he could draw a bigger crowd than Everton can on a Saturday afternoon. **99**

**BILL SHANKLY**

*at Dixie Dean's funeral*

**"**I'm a people's man.
Only the people matter.**"**

**BILL SHANKLY**

**❝**There's Man United and Man City at the bottom of Division One. And by God they'll take some shifting. **❞**

**BILL SHANKLY**

*looking at the League table early in the 1972/3 season*

**"**I was the best manager in Britain because I was never devious or cheated anyone. I'd break my wife's legs if I played against her, but I'd never cheat her.**"**

**BILL SHANKLY**

**"**Some people believe football is a matter of life and death. I am very disappointed with that attitude. I can assure you it is much more important than that.**"**

**BILL SHANKLY**

**"**It wasn't her wedding anniversary, it was her birthday, because there's no way I'd have got married in the football season. And it wasn't Rochdale. It was Rochdale Reserves.**"**

**BILL SHANKLY**

*refuting stories that he had taken his wife Nessie to watch Rochdale on their wedding anniversary*

**66** Some people might think we are lazy, but that's fine. What's the point of tearing players to pieces in the first few days? We never bothered with sand dunes and hills and roads; we trained on grass, where football is played. **99**

**BILL SHANKLY**

*on pre-season training*

**"** Take that poof bandage off, and what do you mean you've hurt your knee? It's Liverpool's knee! **"**

**BILL SHANKLY**

*to an injured Tommy Smith*

**❝**Now, boys, Crerand's deceptive, he's slower than you think. **❞**

**BILL SHANKLY**

*preparing for a meeting with Paddy Crerand and Manchester United*

**"**I want to build a team that's invincible, so they'll have to send a team from Mars to beat us.**"**

**BILL SHANKLY**

**"**Matt has got a bad back. I tell you it's two bad backs! And not much of a midfield either.**"**

**BILL SHANKLY**

*putting the boot into Matt Busby's Manchester United*

**"** Chairman Mao has never seen such a show of red strength in all his life. **"**

**BILL SHANKLY**

*addressing 300,000 fans as the 1974 FA Cup
is paraded through the streets of Liverpool*

**66** Liverpool was made for me and
I was made for Liverpool. **99**

**BILL SHANKLY**

# CHAPTER 3

# RED STARS

**❝**I remember as a new boy looking forward to my first Friday team meeting with some anticipation, so imagine my surprise when Tommy Smith sat down a few chairs away, put his feet up and unfolded his copy of the *Sporting Life*. I was waiting for the sparks to fly but no, Bob just got on with his chat and left Smithy to get on with picking the next day's winners.**❞**

**PHIL NEAL**

**❝**With him at centre-half, we could play
Arthur Askey in goal! **❞**

**BILL SHANKLY**
*on Ron Yeats*

**"** Tommy Smith wasn't born,
he was quarried. **"**

**DAVID COLEMAN**

**ff** Stevie Nicol, who I played with at Liverpool, was one of the great utility players and now there is another at Anfield in James Milner." **JJ**

**JAMIE REDKNAPP**

**"** He's just stepped out of the shower. Come in and see him…have a walk round him. He's a colossus. **"**

**BILL SHANKLY**

*unveiling 6ft 2in, 14-stone centre-half Ron Yeats to journalists*

**The White Pele? You're more like the White Nellie!**

**BILL SHANKLY**

*as Peter Thompson struggled to reproduce his international form in Brazil on the domestic stage*

**❝**Yes, he misses a few.
But he gets in the right place
to miss them. **❞**

**BILL SHANKLY**

*on Roger Hunt*

**❝**Keegan had a Doncaster childhood and a Scunthorpe upbringing, yet he seems to have been born with Liverpool in his soul.**❞**

**JOE MERCER**

**"**Muhammad Ali, Tiger Woods, Michael Jordan and Diego Maradona. I prefer Pele to Maradona as a player but I'd have Maradona for the laughs. **"**

**DANIEL STURRIDGE**

*reveals his dream dinner companions*

**"**Strikers are selfish, at least the very best are. It's not about giving everyone else a chance as far as you are concerned. You want to be out there on the pitch scoring goals. It proves you are a winner.**"**

**IAN RUSH**

**"** He was like a fox in that area, the way he hunted for his goals. **"**

**❝** Who can say what he's going to do? It's a talent and you can't teach it, you can't coach it. All you can do is enjoy it. **❞**

**ROY EVANS**

*discussing a young Robbie Fowler*

**❝**I always have my packet of chocolate buttons.**❞**

**PETER BEARDSLEY**

*explaining the secret of his success*

**❝** A good skipper, but he could
have been a really great one if he
had been a bit more extrovert. **❞**

**BOB PAISLEY**

*summing up Alan Hansen*

**❝**I'd have to say Steven Gerrard has been
the biggest influence on my career so far.
I watched him when I was younger and then
to go and play and train with him every day
was massive for me.**❞**

**JORDAN HENDERSON**

**ff** Robbie Fowler's from the South End of Liverpool, like myself. People from that part of the world need to be tough to survive and make a name for themselves. And believe me, Robbie is tough. **ff**

**JOHN ALDRIDGE**

**"**I always try to be quick in possession, whether that's running with the ball, playing a quick pass or trying a trick. I really like to dribble with the ball, and that's my role in the team.**"**

**PHILIPPE COUTINHO**

**"**He's a walking advert for the benefits of junk food. He'll eat five packets of crisps and wash it down with Coke and Mars bars.**"**

**MARK LAWRENSON**

*weighs up Steve Nicol's diet*

**❝**He was struggling… he was probably too unselfish at the time. That's often the case with a young player, particularly one coming into a successful side. He tended to look for others and lay the ball off when he could have had a go himself. I told him to be a bit more selfish, and it wasn't long before the penny dropped.**❞**

**BOB PAISLEY**

*recalling Ian Rush's goal drought when he first arrived at Anfield*

**❝**I realise now that computer games have affected my performance badly. The last time I had a nightmare was at Middlesbrough in the Coca-Cola Cup and I had played Nintendo for eight hours beforehand.**❞**

**DAVID JAMES**

**"** People don't realise that getting married, which Robbie did in the summer, and becoming a family man can affect you. It's a hell of a transition which can have dramatic consequences. I remember Bob Paisley used to say you would have to forget players for up to 12 months if they had just got married and had children. **"**

**IAN RUSH**

**❝**I never saw anyone in this country to touch him. I can think of only two who could go ahead of him – Pele and possibly Cruyff. **❞**

**GRAEME SOUNESS**

*on Kenny Dalglish*

**"**Young Gerrard has the world at his feet. For that age, he's some player, but even now, he could go anywhere, do anything.**"**

**BOBBY ROBSON**

**“**Steven Gerrard is Souness
with pace and that's a hell of a player. **”**

**ALAN HANSEN**

**"**If you ask any of the lads, I think I can have a laugh just like any other 20-year-old. But at certain times I think you've got to be serious and have your head screwed on.**"**

**MICHAEL OWEN**

**"**When you're having a tough time as a team, you all need to stay together. You cannot start becoming individuals.**"**

**ADAM LALLANA**

**"**Footballers are recognised everywhere we go. We were in Dublin once, just doing a bit of shopping, and were mobbed in the street. It was like a scene out of a Beatles movie; we had to run to jump into a cab to escape. Another time I was even recognised on the Great Wall of China!**"**

**STEVE MCMANAMAN**

**❝** McManaman was a very deceptive player and to see him move on the field you wouldn't think he was travelling as fast as he was. It was only when you saw him outstrip people that you realised how fast he was. **❞**

**ERIC SUTCLIFFE**

*former Secretary of the Liverpool Schools FA*

**❝**I hate training, I hate running, but at Liverpool they say: if you don't put it in at training, how do you expect to put it in during a match?**❞**

**ROBBIE FOWLER**

*1996*

**“**You have to accept Luis for what he is.
When he played for me at Tenerife, I tried
to change him, but you have to say OK,
he does what he does and provides
different things. **”**

**RAFA BENITEZ**

*on the highly talented but unpredictable Luis Garcia*

**❝**Of course with Phil's skills, everyone wants to give him the ball and wait for something special to happen. Then you think, 'oh no, don't shoot again.' But if I could shoot like he could shoot, then I would try it all the time. **❞**

**JURGEN KLOPP**

*on Philippe Coutinho*

**❝**There's a famous saying in my country, 'O Brasileiro Nao Desiste Nunca,' which means Brazilians never give up. It is a sentence I like and a view I take for life.**❞**

**PHILIPPE COUTINHO**

**❝**He can pass, he can tackle, he can do almost anything you put to him. The manager at Liverpool keeps telling him he can get better. If he can, he'll be a frightening sight.**❞**

**PETER CROUCH**

*on Steven Gerrard, September 2006*

**❝**Is he the best in the world?
He might not get the attention of
Messi and Ronaldo but yes,
I think he might be.**❞**

**ZINEDINE ZIDANE**

*on Steven Gerrard, March 2009*

# CHAPTER 4

# THE KOP ON TOP

**"** Three-one in your Cup final. **"**

*Victorious* **LIVERPOOL FANS'** *chant to Everton*
*following the 3–1 win at Goodison in September 2001*

**"** For those of you watching in black and white, Liverpool are the team with the ball. **"**

**LIVERPOOL FANS**

*joke before the 1984 Milk Cup final with Everton*

**"**The Kop was the best place in the world to watch football as you were surrounded by so many characters and passionate people. There used to be a bloke called 'the Mad Brickie' who kept us all entertained by getting on the pitch at half-time.**"**

**RICKY TOMLINSON**

**ff** The Kop's exclusive, an institution, and if you're a member of the Kop you feel you're a member of a society, you've got thousands of friends around you and they're united and loyal. **JJ**

**BILL SHANKLY**

**ff** That first night was the greatest.
We were in the front row of the Kemlyn
stand. The whole time my eyes were fixed
on the Kop. I couldn't believe it. I was
mesmerised. The steam was rising and
the noise was incredible. **JJ**

**PHIL THOMPSON**

*remembering his first visit to Anfield at the age of 11*

**❝**The whole of my life, what they wanted was honesty. They were not so concerned with cultured football, but with triers who gave one hundred per cent. **❞**

**BOB PAISLEY**

*on the Kop*

**❝**Tell me ma, me ma,
To put the champagne on ice,
We're going to Cardiff twice,
Tell me ma, me ma.**❞**

**LIVERPOOL FANS**

*to the tune of 'Que Sera' in celebration of their return trip to the
Millennium Stadium for a Cup Final during the historic
Treble season of 2000–01*

**“** When the ball's down the Kop end, they frighten the ball. Sometimes they suck it into the back of the net. **”**

**BILL SHANKLY**

**❝**I would just love to have gone
and stood in the Kop. **❞**

**KENNY DALGLISH**

**"**You had to be strong to be on the Kop. When I was about 13, I tried to go in the middle where all the excitement was and almost got cut in half. I was only 5ft 7in. A big docker pushed the crowd back and I ducked out and went back to my usual place to the left of the goal. **"**

**ELVIS COSTELLO**

**66** There's no noise like the Anfield
noise and I love it! **99**

**IAN ST JOHN**

**❝**The highlight of the game was not our two goals or the three points we won. It was when our fans made the Kop sing 'You'll Never Walk Alone'. It was as if they couldn't come here and go home without hearing it sung in all its glory. It was very emotional, and something I'll remember forever.**❞**

**KEVIN KEEGAN**

*after Newcastle's 2–0 win at Anfield, 1994*

# CHAPTER 5

# INSIDE THE
# BOOT ROOM

**"**I remember Jimmy Adamson crowing after Burnley had beaten us that his players were in a different league. At the end of the season they were.**"**

**BOB PAISLEY**

**"**Sometimes if you spit up in the air, it can come back in your face.**"**

**GERARD HOULLIER**

reacting to jibes from Crystal Palace's Clinton Morrison after

*the first leg of the 2001 Worthington Cup semi-final*

**"**He was only an ordinary sized man, but he just had this presence, he used to stand so tall. When he stood in front of the Kop he had thousands in the palms of his hands.**"**

**RICKY TOMLINSON**

*in praise of Bill Shankly*

**"**When I left school, the head said,
'I hope you can do something in football
because, if not, I have not the best
feeling for your future.'**"**

JURGEN KLOPP

**"** They say he's tough, he's hard, he's ruthless. Rubbish, he's got a heart of gold, he loves the game, he loves his fans, he loves his players. He's like an old collie dog, he doesn't like hurting his sheep. He'll drive them. Certainly. But bite them, never. **"**

**JOE MERCER**

*on Bill Shankly*

**If Bill had one failing, it was the fact that he did not like to upset players that had done so well for him. He was a softie at heart.**

**BOB PAISLEY**

**"** I am not going to call myself anything. I am a normal guy from the Black Forest. My mother is watching this press conference at home. If you are going to call me anything, call me the 'Normal One'. **"**

**JURGEN KLOPP**

**❝**I love challenges. I like the aggravation that goes with football management.**❞**

**GRAEME SOUNESS**

*taking over at Anfield, 1991*

**❝**You have to feel a defeat. You cannot say 'I don't care, it's not important.' You always have to strike back. We can say all of these things, but you know you can fall down and then you have to stand up. That's the truth, but it's completely normal – only silly idiots stay on the floor and wait for the next defeat. **❞**

**JURGEN KLOPP**

**"I have only felt like this once before, and that was when my father died, because Bill was like a second father to me."**

KEVIN KEEGAN

*hearing of Bill Shankly's death*

**"**When Bob appeared on television the public saw this guy with the wide grin on his face and that quaint Geordie accent which I could never really understand. He was like everybody's favourite uncle. But there was a completely ruthless streak in Bob. If he decided that a player had to be axed, then that was that. Sentiment did not come into it.**"**

**ALAN HANSEN**

**"**I spent the first year on a good horse, but I was like an apprentice riding the Derby favourite. I was cautious and went too wide round the bends. We should have won the Championship.**"**

**BOB PAISLEY**

**"**He was a great man.
His motivation could move mountains.**"**

**RON YEATS'S**

*tribute to Bill Shankly*

**❝**Bill Shankly set such a high standard. Liverpool have been geared to this sort of thing for 15 years. I have just helped things along.**❞**

**BOB PAISLEY**

*winning his first title*

**"**He's broken that silly myth that nice
guys don't win anything. **"**

**BRIAN CLOUGH**

*assessing Bob Paisley's triumphs*

**"** He, Joe Fagan and Ronnie Moran give the club that homely appearance, but beneath what might seem a soft exterior there is a hard centre. **"**

**JIMMY ARMFIELD**

*considering Bob Paisley's inner steel*

**❝I never wanted the job in the first place.❞**

**BOB PAISLEY**

**❝**I'm too old and tired. It's a job for a young man's brains and energy. It's not an eight-hours-a-day-job, it's twenty-four hours a day. And there's no way you can get away from that.**❞**

*64-year-old* **JOE FAGAN**

*stepping down as manager*

**❝**Our job is to make the fans happy. When we win, 45,000 people go home happy. When we lose, it not only affects them, it affects the cat. **❞**

**GERARD HOULLIER**

**"** It's like any relationship. Sometimes it goes wrong and you simply have to work at putting it right again. There's no point trying to pretend it's perfect all the time. We don't sit here holding hands seven days a week. **"**

**ROY EVANS**

*on his partnership with Gerard Houllier*

**❝** The best band in the world. My mother said it, my father said it: Number one – The Beatles. **❞**

**JURGEN KLOPP**

**" Reputations do not mean anything to me. If they did, I would choose Ian Rush and Roger Hunt up front. "**

**GERARD HOULLIER**

**"**Shankly gave the players and the city their pride and passion back. If you didn't have the pride and the passion, then you didn't play for Shankly and you didn't play for Liverpool.**"**

**FAN RICKY TOMLINSON**

**"** It's not about the long ball or the short ball, it's about the right ball. **"**

**BOB PAISLEY**

**"**Even Ian Callaghan had to bend down to get through the door after one of Shankly's team talks. It was amazing how he could build you up.**"**

**RON YEATS**

**❝**We didn't know what he was talking about half the time but we knew what he wanted.**❞**

**TOMMY SMITH**

*trying to follow Bob Paisley's mangled English*

**"**Bob would call us together on a
Friday morning and usually just say
'The same team as last week',
and we would get on with it. **"**

**MARK LAWRENSON**

**❝**I don't know what will happen when he goes full-time! **❞**

**BOBBY ROBSON**

*on Kenny Dalglish's success as player/manager, 1988*

121

**"** What do I say to them in the dressing-room? Nothing really. Most of the time I don't even know what they are going to do myself. **"**

**KENNY DALGLISH**

**❝** There is no way a game of football is more important than grieving. **❞**

**KENNY DALGLISH**

*puts things into perspective by leaving Craig Bellamy out of the side on the day fellow Welshman Gary Speed was found dead*

**❝**I think what he does is a model for other managers around the world – it's a perfect model for all the kids as well. As for the style of football, even Barcelona are now copying his style.**❞**

**RAFA BENITEZ**

*gives a tongue-in-cheek appraisal of Sam Allardyce*

**"** Go compare! Go compare! **"**

**WEST HAM FANS**

*chant to Rafa*

**"**Just a thought! Woke up with Liverpool manager lying beside me! Twenty years since that happened!**"**

**MARINA DALGLISH**

*tweets her excitement*

**❝**You know I could have stayed in my comfortable chair in South Wales having the first Welsh team that got promoted and been there a number of years, but for me I wanted to work at a club that was world class and at the very, very top.**❞**

**BRENDAN RODGERS**

# CHAPTER 6

# COMINGS
# AND GOINGS

**❝**When I went to see the chairman to tell him, it was like walking to the electric chair.**❞**

**BILL SHANKLY**

*on his decision to quit*

**"**I had to say I was retiring,
though I believe you retire when
you're in a coffin and the lid is
nailed down and your name
is on it. **"**

**BILL SHANKLY**

**"** Don't you recognise him? This man is the future captain of England. **"**

**BILL SHANKLY**

*to a traffic policeman who had stopped him on his way back*
*to Liverpool with new signing, Emlyn Hughes*

**❝**I knew this was the right club for me.
I always had a good feeling about moving to
Liverpool. I am happy to be a part of it.
I feel blessed.**❞**

**GEORGINIO WIJNALDUM**

**"**Kenny Dalglish was the reason I signed for Liverpool. It was his reputation and his stature in the game that persuaded me and the fact that he gave me a particularly smart pair of boots. It is the only 'bung' I have ever received. They were two sizes too big for me, but I didn't half look good in them.**"**

**STEVE MCMANAMAN**

**❝**I know that Jamie Carragher is a legend here in Liverpool and hopefully I will be as well. I want to be a legend one day. That's why I try always to give my best. **❞**

**EMRE CAN**

**"** There's not many
around like me. **"**

**PETER CROUCH**

*on signing for Liverpool, overtaking 6ft 6in goalkeeper*
*Chris Kirkland as the tallest Reds player ever by exactly one inch*

**“**Playing Roma in Rome in the European Cup final and scoring a penalty in the shoot-out to help us win it. That was my very last kick for Liverpool and it doesn't really get any better than that. **”**

**GRAEME SOUNESS**

**❝**Management is a seven-days-a-week job. The intensity of it takes its toll on your health. Some people want to go on for ever, and I obviously don't.**❞**

**KENNY DALGLISH**

*1991*

**❝**The chief executive, Peter Robinson, and I had just sat down at our fortnightly meeting with the manager when he came out and said he wanted to finish. I jokingly said: 'This afternoon?' and he said: 'Yes'.**❞**

*Liverpool chairman* **NOEL WHITE**
*reeling from Kenny Dalglish's shock departure*

**"**He is a perfectionist and so everyone wants to be like him. You want to give perfection during training and give 100 per cent on the pitch. It is great to see how intense he is on the touchline. He is really emotional and shows that in every part of the game.**"**

**DEJAN LOVREN**

*on Jurgen Klopp*

**"** He is the best player that
Liverpool have signed this century.
It was the best decision we have ever made.
He sets such a fine example, not just to our
players but to everybody in the game. **"**

Chairman **JOHN SMITH**

*praising Kenny Dalglish as Liverpool clinch the League title in 1986*

**"** Are we talking about a change of religion here or just a change of football club? **"**

**GERARD HOULLIER**

*over fears that Nick Barmby may have had to go into*
*hiding following his move across Stanley Park*

**"**I'm delighted that he has signed. I think he's one of the top strikers in world football.**"**

**BRENDAN RODGERS**

*on Luis Suarez, after the Uruguayan entered into a new long-term*
*contract following the London 2012 Olympic Games football tournament*

**❝**Liverpool have gone backwards and the players he has brought in just haven't worked. I think unfortunately Roy was the wrong man at the wrong time for Liverpool and it has been a case of thanks but no thanks.**❞**

**MARK LAWRENSON**

*on Hodgson's departure*

**"** I have always wanted to come back and it has been a long time but I'm glad to say I'm back now. Leaving was probably one of my biggest regrets I have had in football. I'm chuffed to bits. I can't really believe it's happened again so I'm ecstatic. **"**

*Kop favourite* **ROBBIE FOWLER**
*rejoins Liverpool, January 2006*

# CHAPTER 7

# SECRETS
# OF SUCCESS

**"** Tommy Smith would start
a riot in a graveyard. **"**

**BILL SHANKLY**

**❝**When you see Tommy Smith go down,
then you know he's been hurt. **❞**

**BOB PAISLEY**

**❝**We do things together. I'd walk into the toughest dockside pub in the world with this lot because you know that if things got tough, nobody would 'bottle' it and scoot off.**❞**

**EMLYN HUGHES**

*on his Liverpool team-mates*

**If** I told people that the secret of Liverpool's success is a dip in the Mersey three times a week, I not only reckon they'd believe me but I think our river would be full of footballers from all over the country. **"**

Club trainer **RONNIE MORAN**

**There's** so many clubs been ruined by people's ego. The day after we won our first European Cup, we were back at this club at 9.45 in the morning, talking about how we would do it again, working from that moment, because nobody has the right to win anything they haven't earned. **"**

**BOB PAISLEY**

**❝**Bottle is a quality too, you know. It's not just about ball control and being clever. Sometimes you have to show the world what's between your legs.**❞**

GRAEME SOUNESS

**"**I love tackling. It's better than sex.
A great tackle gets everybody
pumped up. **"**

**PAUL INCE**

**"** To be the best you have to forget the partying and concentrate all your energies on the football. **"**

MICHAEL OWEN

**"**I'm not allowed to wear gloves. When I was about 12, my dad came to watch me play. I brought a pair of gloves out and he walked off!**"**

**STEVEN GERRARD**

**❝**Liverpool players must play like a lion, give his all. There must be determination, commitment and resolve to be a Liverpool player. **❞**

GERARD HOULLIER

# CHAPTER 8

# MAGIC MOMENTS

**"**We wore the all red strip for the first time. Christ, the players looked like giants. And we played like giants. **"**

**BILL SHANKLY**

*after Liverpool had worn their all-red kit for the first time, against Anderlecht at Anfield, 25 November 1964*

**❝**Getting the Nou Camp booing
their own players because they
didn't touch the ball in the
first ten minutes.**❞**

**EMLYN HUGHES**

recalling his favourite moment from Liverpool's triumphant 1976
*UEFA Cup run – a semi-final trip to Barcelona*

**“** This is the greatest night in Liverpool's history. This is the result of planning, of simplicity, of how to play the game in a simple manner. I think the whole world realises that it's the way to play. **”**

**BILL SHANKLY**

*after watching the 1977 European Cup final*

**"**I was really confident. I took a penalty in training and put it in the same spot. Just like that.**"**

**ALAN KENNEDY**

*after scoring the winning penalty in the*
*European Cup Final shoot-out against Roma in 1984*

**❝**As the ball came over, I remembered what Graham Taylor said about my having no right foot, so I headed it in.**❞**

**JOHN BARNES**

*scoring against Taylor's Aston Villa in a 1988 FA Cup tie*

**"**When you play in a European final, you are looking for immortality. People remember who was playing and when you look at programmes from finals you just recall the facts of the game. These boys have produced a game which will be remembered for a long time.**"**

**GERARD HOULLIER**

*after the 2001 UEFA Cup final*

**❝** For far too long our fans have had to see a team in the backwaters of English football, so it is great to have people talking about Liverpool again. **❞**

**PHIL THOMPSON**

*celebrating the 2001 treble*

**"** I think the game will be a dull 0–0. **"**

**JORDI CRUYFF**

*of Alaves before the UEFA Cup Final*
*which Liverpool won 5–4, May 2001*

**“**I thought it was a bit cruel of Liverpool to put Steven Gerrard on when we were getting tired!**”**

*Total Network Solutions boss* **KEN MCKENNA** *after his club's 3–0 defeat at Anfield in the qualifying round of the Champions League, July 2005*

**❝I just wanted to jump into the stand and start celebrating with those wonderful fans. ❞**

**STEVEN GERRARD**

*on overcoming Chelsea in the 2005 Champions League semi-final*

**❝**Liverpool produced one of the greatest comebacks in the history of football. They created for themselves an utter disaster and somehow turned a lost match around in six impossible minutes... The tide turned in a manner that defied logical and even tactical sense. It was simply as if God had changed sides.**❞**

**SIMON BARNES**

*in The Times on the 2005 Champions League Final*

**"**Amazing, astounding, awe-inspiring, breathtaking, extraordinary, hair-raising, heart-stirring, magnificent, marvellous, miraculous, moving, overwhelming, spectacular, spine-tingling, striking, stunning, stupefying, stupendous, wonderful.**"**

**LIVERPOOL FC'S OFFICIAL WEBSITE**

*on the Reds' great fightback*

**"**Carra came up to me like he was crazy. He grabbed me and said, 'Jerzy, Jerzy, Jerzy – remember Bruce [Grobbelaar]? He did crazy things in 1984. You have to do the same.' He told me I would be the hero.**"**

**JERZY DUDEK**

*on what he called his 'starfish with jelly legs' routine during the Champions League Final penalty shoot-out*

172

**❝**We talked at half-time and told the players that we needed to believe. We started to press with more energy and the belief came back. I was so proud of my players in extra-time – this was the greatest night I've had as a manager.**❞**

**RAFA BENITEZ**

**"** I'm on top of the world.
This is the best night of my life. **"**

**STEVEN GERRARD**

*after holding aloft the European Cup, May 2005*

**❝**I just can't believe the scenes around here.**❞**

*Anfield steward* **PHIL LYE** *on the Champions League victory as a man in his twenties, naked but for a pair of socks and a large flag, was seen running along the streets of terraced houses near the stadium info*

**❝It was difficult to say we deserved to win or the other team. It was a magnificent Final.❞**

**RAFA BENITEZ**

*celebrates lifting the FA Cup, after a penalty shoot-out, May 2006*

**❝**I don't know when the last time we were there was, but we know where we are going. We've maybe forgotten the route because we've not been there for a while, but I'm sure the driver will remember.**❞**

**KENNY DALGLISH**

*relishing Liverpool's first trip to Wembley since 1996*

**"**Steven Gerrard could play right-back and still be effective because these are world-class players. I wish he had been at right-back though!**"**

*Burnley boss* **OWEN COYLE**

*after seeing his side hammered by Liverpool, September 2009*

**"** Well, the bell might not quite be tolling for Real Madrid, but there is a man wearing earplugs preparing to climb the tower. **"**

*ESPN commentator* **ADRIAN HEALEY**

*as Liverpool overwhelm Real 5–0 on aggregate, March 2009*

**❝I kicked every ball tonight. I'm more tired now than when I play! ❞**

*Injured* **STEVEN GERRARD**

*after watching the 4–4 draw with Arsenal in a TV studio, April 2009*

**180**

**❝**I think anyone who has ever won a trophy, whether it's at Wembley or wherever, has come away and said, 'I enjoyed that, I'd love to do it again'.**❞**

**KENNY DALGLISH**

*after Liverpool had won the Carling Cup, 2012*

# CHAPTER 9

# YOU'LL NEVER WALK ALONE

**"**I've been on this planet for 45 years, and have supported Liverpool for 42 of them.**"**

**ROY EVANS**

*becoming manager in 1994*

**❝**He was the same as me, a Liverpool fan from a council estate who loved his footy and kicked a ball around in the street.**❞**

**STEVEN GERRARD**

*remembering his cousin, Jon-Paul Gilhooley,*
*who died in the Hillsborough tragedy, aged 10*

**❝**The fans were the innocent victims of a tragedy caused by the criminal neglect of the people you believed were there to protect you. But for 23 years the fans were portrayed as responsible for the disaster, effectively branded murderers. **❞**

**ROBBIE FOWLER**

*reacts to the Hillsborough Independent Panel's report*

**❝**To an awful lot of people, now you understand why we couldn't just get over it.**❞**

**PHIL THOMPSON**

*on Twitter*

**If we had to lose our record, I'd sooner it be against Liverpool than anyone else.**

*Newcastle boss* **KEVIN KEEGAN** *as Liverpool became the first team that season to take a point at St James' Park, 1994*

**❝**Worldwide, Liverpool's a club that is renowned throughout. I think you go to wherever, Kuala Lumpur, New Zealand, as far away as you can, everyone knows about Liverpool.**❞**

**BRENDAN RODGERS**

*just before his first Merseyside derby, 2012*

**"**Think my chances of making the Liverpool side are gone now. Might still be able to get a game at one of those London clubs though. **"**

*Liverpool fan* **JOHN PEEL**

*at his 50th birthday party*

**"I love the club, the fans and the city and, with a club like this and supporters like this, I could never say no to staying."**

**RAFA BENITEZ**

*committing himself to Liverpool until 2014*

**"**Walk on, walk on,
With hope in your heart,
And you'll never walk alone,
You'll never walk alone.**"**

**THE KOP CHOIR**

*every home game from 1963 to the present day*